Contents

Day 1 — Do Not Fret

Scripture: Psalm 37:1, *Do not fret because of evildoers, nor be envious of the workers of iniquity.*

Key Thought: Anxiety over evil drains the soul more than evil itself.

Prayer: "Lord, quiet my spirit and anchor my trust in You."

It is no exaggeration to say that we are witnessing, in real time in our nation and world, workers of iniquity. This is not something new, but rarely has it been on full display at a national level among national political leaders as of this writing. We are seeing despotism and dictatorial tactics in a nation where the United States Constitution states that "We The People" are the basis of its form of government – what Abraham Lincoln described as government *"Of the people, by the people, and for the people."*

As we are dealing with many grievous situations in our world, those of us who will not be silent must maintain balance. We must remain vigilant and active. At the same time, we must avoid strife or becoming obsessed with the deeds of evildoers.

The Scripture plainly says, *"do not fret."* As a matter of fact, in Psalm 37 the words *"do not fret"* appear three times. The third mention, in verse 8, states: *"Cease from anger, and forsake wrath; do not fret—it only causes harm."*

So while we who will not be silent, as many others are, must stay engaged. We also have to draw closer to God and keep our hearts clear of wrath, strife, and fretfulness.

One way to avoid fretting is found in spending devotional time with the Lord. and allowing the Holy Spirit to minister peace to our hearts.

Jesus said in John 14:26–27, *"Peace I leave with you, My peace I give to you; not as the world gives do I give to you. Let not your heart be troubled, neither let it be afraid."*

Through this peace, we can steady our troubled hearts, and we will not fear the actions of ungodly people.

Reflection Question: "In what ways, specifically, do I need to stop fretting?"

Day 2 — The Temporary Nature of Evil

Psalm 37:2 *"For they shall soon be cut down like the grass, And wither as the green herb."*

Key Thought: Wicked success is short-lived

Prayer: Help me remember what truly lasts

It is important to recognize that Psalm 37 is a wisdom psalm, not a lament. Some passages in the Bible express the heartbreak of the writer. Here, David is instructing God's people on how to live faithfully when the wicked appear to prosper.

The Hebrew word for "soon" does not necessarily mean immediately. Within a biblical timeframe, "soon" is measured against eternity, not according to our frustration and impatience. This is another reason why we don't want to fret. The prosperity of the wicked that looks stable now is already on a countdown.

The Hebrew word for "cut down" is often used of harvesting or mowing, not violent destruction. The "green herb" mentioned in this text refers to quickly growing plants without a deep root system. Some plants grow fast, and they fade fast. During the summer, we had an abundance of beautiful plants in our yard; now, in the middle of winter, they're all gone. That's how God will ultimately deal with the wicked.

What looks alive is already dying. So we don't want to overreact to wicked people. That's not to say that a civil justice system should not deal with evildoers before God's judgment. This psalm emphasizes the importance of believers not fretting or living in lament and frustration.

Psalm 37 reminds us that evil has visibility, not viability. Wickedness has momentum, not longevity. God does not need to rush judgment—but judgment is certain.

However, remember that in a pluralistic democratic republic, we have both the ability and the duty to resist evil and seek justice. Some believers make the mistake of thinking they should sit back and let God handle everything. That mindset only allows oppressors to hurt people more.

Encourage yourself in the Lord by keeping these realities in your heart and mind.

Reflection Question: What things that you thought would happen "soon" need to be reevaluated in light of God's timing?

Day 3 — Trust & Do Good

Psalm 37:3, *Trust in the Lord, and do good;*
Dwell in the land, and feed on His faithfulness.

Key Thought: Trust in God must be accompanied by faithful action.

Prayer: Teach me to trust You through faithful living.

As previously stated, Psalm 37 is a psalm of wisdom. David is not lamenting injustice as much as he is instructing God's people on how to live faithfully when evil seems to prosper.

There are four commands from the Lord in this text. Remember that whatever God requires, He provides.

Command #1: "Trust in the LORD."

The Hebrew verb "trust" means to place full confidence in the Lord and rely on His security. Trusting God is relational and lifelong, not just a transaction for the moment.

Trust is the foundation of righteous living. Everything flows out of confidence in God's character. He is trustworthy!

Command #2: "Do good."

The Hebrew verb "do good" speaks of active, intentional righteousness—ethical living, generosity, justice, and faithfulness in everyday life. There is nothing passive about doing good. It cannot be done in isolation, only among people.

This is how we overcome the effects of evil in our world—we do good.

Command #3: "Dwell in the land."

We know our ultimate "land" is with the Lord, but while living in this present time, we are to dwell in the land of God's promise, provision, and presence. The idea behind the word dwell is to settle, remain, or abide—not merely pass through.

Trusting God means we refuse to abandon our God-given place, calling, or responsibility, regardless of the circumstances we face.

Command #4: "Feed on His faithfulness."

The Hebrew verb "feed" means to graze, to shepherd, or to be nourished.

The word faithfulness refers to God's steadfastness, reliability, firmness, and truth.

The picture is of a person who is continually nourished by God's dependable character, much like sheep grazing in a secure pasture. Some translations render this phrase as "enjoy safe pasture" (NIV), emphasizing sustained provision and security.

Christ-followers do not feed on fear, outrage, or comparison, but on the proven faithfulness of God.

God is faithful!

Reflection Question: How do the four "*commands*" speak to you?

Day 4 — Delight in the Lord

Psalm 37:4 *Delight yourself also in the Lord, and He shall give you the desires of your heart.*

Key Thought: God reshapes desires before fulfilling them.

Prayer: Align my heart's desires with Yours.

Delighting in the Lord reshapes our heart so that what God does is not the fulfillment of personal wants, but rather desires that have been transformed by God. The things I "desired" before walking with Jesus are very different from when I began walking with the Lord.

The biblical meaning of "delight" means *to take pleasure in, to incline toward, or to bend.* Our delight is known by the things we take pleasure in, are inclined toward, or that bend us. That can be something positive or something negative. Therefore, we must pay attention to our desires and judge whether we are motivated by God or by something else.

Delighting in the Lord is more than inclining, or bending, toward circumstances, success, or outcomes. We delight in the Lord Himself – His character, presence, and promises. Life with God is relational, not transactional.

What comes out of becoming "bent" through our relationship

with God is being granted, bestowed, and entrusted with our genuine desires of the heart. The Lord wants to do all the things He has put into our hearts. We just need to get out of our own way.

This verse is often misunderstood as a blank check for personal wishes. However, the promise is conditional in a "formative" sense. We are being formed by our interactions with God. For this reason, it is important to purify and clarify our desires and delights.

As we delight in the Lord, our heart is shaped. We open the door for Jesus to refine, align, and calibrate our hearts. What we grow to desire increasingly reflects God's will.

Psalm 37:4 teaches that fulfillment does not come from chasing desires, but from delighting in God. When God becomes the joy of our heart, He provides what that renewed heart desires. This comes from the Lord and flows from Him toward us.

Reflection Question: How have my desires and delights changed?

Day 5 — Commit Your Way

Psalm 37:5, *Commit your way to the Lord, Trust also in Him, And He shall bring it to pass.*

Key Thought: Surrender outcomes to God.

Prayer: I place my path fully in Your hands.

To commit "your way" carries the idea of rolling a burden off yourself and placing it onto another. This is not a single decision, but an entire course of our lives, our plans, direction, and daily conduct.

Committing here is not a passive decision; it is an intentional transfer of ownership. We are choosing to place our path under God's authority rather than manage it by ourselves.

By "trusting," we reinforce the first command to commit. Without trust in the Lord, we are left with ritual and religion. Trust involves confidence, security, and reliance based on God's proven character.

Commitment is the act, and trust is the posture of the heart that sustains it. Trust assumes God is both able and faithful. The result of committing and trusting the Lord is this: *"And He shall bring it to pass."*

This speaks of God's action, not human effort. We may not experience instant results or a pain-free process, but we have the assurance of God's will and wisdom being carried out in His time.

Faith in God is a transfer of control. When we roll our lives onto the Lord and trust Him, we are freed from manipulation, fretfulness, and self-reliance

Reflection Question: What are you still carrying that God has asked you to roll onto Him?

Day 6 — God Will Vindicate

Psalm 37:6, *"He shall bring forth your righteousness as the light, And your justice as the noonday."*

Key Thought: Righteousness does not need self-promotion.

Prayer: Defend my life according to Your will.

God is the One who causes you to come "forth." The phrase "bring forth" speaks of revealing, causing to emerge, or making visible. What God is doing in your life may be misunderstood, and you may face false accusations, but that doesn't matter. God sees the "real you," and He will bring forth your righteous life.

Righteousness and justice are related terms. In fact, they are often used interchangeably.

We don't need to self-promote or try to force recognition. God does the vindication; we only have to maintain our integrity and live in truth.

"Light" speaks of clarity, exposure, and truth. What is aligned with God cannot be burdened by darkness. God's light in your life will eventually be seen for what it is.

Righteousness is not self-generated. Jesus is our righteousness: "But of Him you are in Christ Jesus, who became for us wisdom from God—and righteousness and sanctification and redemption." (1 Corinthians 1:30)

"Your Justice as the Noonday"

"Noonday" represents the brightest point of the day. Justice is light, and injustice is darkness. The Lord is a God of justice, and He works for the vindication of people who are mistreated and oppressed. We should do the same.

Justice may be delayed in recognition, but it is never denied. God's justice is not hidden, rushed, or incomplete—it is thorough and unmistakable.

Psalm 37:6 assures us that what is right will be revealed, and what is just will be made clear.

Reflection Question: In what ways does God bring forth righteousness and justice?

Day 7 — Loosen Your Grip on Anger

Psalm 37:8, *Cease from anger, and forsake wrath; Do not fret—it only causes harm.*

Key Thought: Unchecked anger corrodes the soul.

Prayer: Cleanse my heart of bitterness.

Some circumstances that we face in the United States, and others face in the larger world, are very grievous, disturbing, and unjust. We are called by the Lord to respond through prayer, rebuking oppressors, and helping affected people.

We can be right about injustice and still be wrong in our response. However, silence is not the appropriate response to evil and injustice. This is why we must seek the Lord to maintain balance in our approach.

"Cease from anger"

The Hebrew word "cease" means "loosening the grip." Those of us who serve others and care about what affects vulnerable people often have a firm grip on these concerns. We may have a justified form of anger. What we do not want is to grip anger so tightly that our emotions and judgment become distorted.

There is a form of anger that goes beyond a useful motivating emotion and becomes irritation that lingers and shapes our behavior in adverse ways.

"Forsake wrath"

"Wrath" is another level of anger that involves rage and burning fury, which is never helpful. Wrath is unchecked anger that comes from emotional escalation. David shows the progression: unchecked anger → inflamed wrath → destructive action.

This is part of the motivation for rioting. When justified anger becomes mixed with a lack of emotional control, it leads to rage and burning fury. At that point, emotions take over and people act out of control, causing harm.

"Do not fret, it only causes harm"

Fretting is anxious, agitated preoccupation that keeps the mind fixated. Fretting fuels resentment, impatience, impulsive reactions, and loss of spiritual perspective.

Jesus said in John 14:26–27, *"Peace I leave with you, My peace I give to you; not as the world gives do I give to you. Let not your heart be troubled, neither let it be afraid."*

He also said in Matthew 11:28, *"Come to Me, all you who labor and are heavy laden, and I will give you rest."*

Psalm 37:8 teaches that unchecked anger and fretfulness distort judgment, damage character, and lead to harmful outcomes.

All the more reason to lean into God so that we can remain at peace and balanced while being active in serving God, rebuking oppressors, and helping people

.

Reflection Question: In what ways do you need to "loosen your grip" on anger without withdrawing and going silent?

Day 8 — Waiting with Hope & Active Faith

Psalm 37:9, *For evildoers shall be cut off; But those who wait on the Lord, They shall inherit the earth.*

Key Thought: God's purpose is our greatest asset

Prayer: Teach me how to wait on what You are preparing

"Evildoers shall be cut off"

The Hebrew phrase "cut off" speaks of severance, removal, or loss of standing. In covenant language, "cut off" means exclusion from blessing. It does not necessarily mean death.

The focus of this text is the unsustainable nature of evil. The history of the world has seen many evil persons, governments (such as Nazi Germany), and evil deeds. Along with the blessings of God we see the perils of life and people of bad will.

Biblically, "evildoers" are those who act unjustly, oppress others, prosper through wrongdoing, and benefit from manipulated systems. Evil involves willful participation in what harms others and dishonors God. Evildoers may flourish for a time, but their influence and works will not endure.

This is not something we can simply pray away. It is something we work on as Christ followers, communities, and citizens. Sometimes Jesus helped people just for the sake of helping people (such as feeding and healing others). He was not always "evangelizing," because His motive was loving and serving people.

"Those who wait on the LORD"

The Hebrew word "wait" means more than time passing. It carries the idea of hope, expectancy, patience, and active faith in God.

We wait and expect because God's power is greater than our power. Our faith is expressed through endurance and obedience to His instructions. Waiting on the Lord is the antidote to fretting. Instead of overreacting to evil, we remain anchored in God's timing and character.

From this place of strength, we can gain wisdom to know what to do. When you are at the airport waiting for a flight, technicians are preparing the airplane and making sure there is nothing impeding your route. When you are waiting, God is working.

"They shall inherit the earth"

"Inherit" is a covenant word. Biblically, inheritance is connected to continuity, belonging, and stability. Jesus said, "I have set before you an open door, and no one can shut it" (Revelation 3:8).

"To inherit the earth" is more than land ownership (which comes later). It is participation in God's ordered world, living within His purposes and enjoying what He provides. These things can happen while we are living on this earth, even among evildoers.

Jesus said, "Blessed are the meek, for they shall inherit the earth" (Matthew 5:5). We do not want to inherit the earth in its present state. We work to make the best of the environments in which we live during our lifetimes. When it is all said and done, there will be a new heaven and a new earth in which we will live and reign with Christ.

For now, our focus is to serve God's purposes in our generation.

Reflection Question: In light of this Scripture and lesson, what does waiting on the Lord mean?

Day 9 — The Way of Meekness

Psalm 37:11, *But the meek shall inherit the earth, And shall delight themselves in the abundance of peace."*

Key Thought: Meekness is strength.

Prayer: Teach me how to have strength under control

Psalm 37 contrasts the wicked and the righteous. Again, David is not lamenting; he is giving instruction to God's people on how to live faithfully when evil seems to prosper.

- The loud are not the lasting.
- The aggressive are not the inheritors.
- The manipulators are not the permanent.

Here is the Hebrew meaning of "the meek:" Humble, lowly, gentle, dependent. This word does not describe a personality temperament; it describes a decision to live with strength under control. Meekness is not weakness.

During a television commercial, Charles Barkley famously said, "The meek may inherit the Earth, but they won't get the ball." This marketing statement reinforces the false narrative that meek people are weak.

In the world of basketball, some may have considered Tim Duncan to be meek, but those who watched him play understood his intensity. He displayed strength under control.

People who are meek are not passive; they have disciplined intensity.

For example, Moses is called "very meek" (Numbers 12:3), yet he confronted Pharaoh. Meekness has authority without aggression.

"And shall delight themselves in the abundance of peace."

The meek actually live at the highest levels of blessing from God because of their commitment to "delight themselves in the Lord." Living in this manner produces an abundance of peace.

What the meek possess:

"Peace" (shalom in Hebrew) - which is completeness, wholeness, harmony, well-being.

"Abundance" - which is overflow, fullness, excess.

Reflection Question: What are examples of how meekness is not weakness?

Day 10 — Use the Power of Another

Psalm 37:7, *Rest in the Lord, and wait patiently for Him; Do not fret because of him who prospers in his way, Because of the man who brings wicked schemes to pass.*

Key Thought: Stillness is an act of faith.

Prayer: Teach me how to rest in You and not fret

"Rest in the LORD"

The Hebrew word for "rest" means to be still, to be quiet.

The book of Hebrews states, "There remains therefore a rest for the people of God. 10 For he who has entered His rest has himself also ceased from his works as God did from His." (4:9–10)

Resting in the Lord is not inactivity. It is relying on a God's power. It is also knowing that when we have done what we were supposed to do, God does the rest. When we are at rest, we do not have inner agitation or fretting.

David wrote God's words, "Be still, and know that I am God." (Psalm 46:10)

"Wait patiently for Him"

The Hebrew word for "wait patiently" carries the idea of intense expectation. We are not passive while waiting; we are exercising confidence and faith in God.

This is the second of three instances in Psalm 37 where the Lord says, "Do not fret" because of evildoers. It is very frustrating to see people and systems bringing wicked schemes to pass. As of this writing, we are seeing it in real time in our nation at the highest levels of government.

As concerned as we should be, and as active as we should be in helping vulnerable people and seeking to curtail harmful policies, we do not want to let anyone or anything distort our disposition. In the words of an old saying, "Don't let other people's hang-ups hang you up." One of the best definitions of resting in the Lord is this: "Use the power of Another."

By the grace of God, the presence of the Holy Spirit, and keeping our mind on the Lord, we will be able to avoid fretting, rest in the Lord's power, and watch Him do amazing things!

Reflection Question: In what specific ways do you need to use the power of Another, the power of God?

Day 11 — God Sustains the Righteous

Contributor: Stacy Williams

Psalm 37:17 (NIV), *For the power of the wicked will be broken, but the Lord upholds the righteous.*

Key Thought: God upholds those who trust Him.

Prayer: Be my strength today.

This verse contrasts the outcome of the wicked with the outcome of the righteous.

"The wicked" are those who are bent on doing evil, at odds with God's standards, rejecting the fear of the Lord, and actively hostile to the things of God. The word wicked can also carry the idea of self-reliance and pride, which frequently motivate their actions.

The wicked operate outside of the Kingdom of God. They are not sustained or rewarded by Him; rather, any strength they appear to have is ultimately broken. They attempt to operate, maneuver, and manipulate within a fallen system through their own hubris. Their strength is unsustainable.

An analogy would be that of unsupported software. Unsupported software no longer receives assistance or updates from its developer. This eventually results in instability and system failure. Similarly, the wicked operate in a fallen system that leads to brokenness. The wealth of the wicked (Psalm 37:16) and the power associated with it will not last because they are functioning in an unsupported system.

Those who have trusted God for salvation have been made righteous through what He has provided (1 Corinthians 1:30). The righteous have right standing with God and walk in integrity among people. In contrast to the wicked, the righteous lean into God and look to Him for sustaining strength.

The righteous operate in the Kingdom of God which is a system fully supported by God Himself. Their actions are motivated by trust and reliance on His strength and ability. As

Psalm 62:6 declares: *"Truly He is my rock and my salvation; He is my fortress, I will not be shaken."*

The righteous are able to stand firmly on the Rock of their salvation and be supported – upheld– by the Lord.

Reflection Question: In what area of your life do you need to rely on the sustaining power of the Lord?

Day 12 — Evil is Self-Destructive

Psalm 37:12, *The wicked plots against the just, And gnashes at him with his teeth. 13 The Lord laughs at him, For He sees that his day is coming. 14 The wicked have drawn the sword And have bent their bow, To cast down the poor and needy, To slay those who are of upright conduct. 15 Their sword shall enter their own heart, And their bows shall be broken.*

Key Thought: Violence ultimately destroys its source.

Prayer: Help me maintain my hope in You.

Remember that Psalm 37 is wisdom instruction, not lament. David contrasts the temporary activity of the wicked with the enduring stability of the righteous. These verses intensify that contrast by describing active hostility, and God's response.

"The wicked plots against the just, And gnashes at him with his teeth."

In our sinful world, we cannot underestimate the depravity of people who are wicked and self-serving. It is our nature to believe the best in people, but there are some, as the Bible highlights, who are wholly committed to taking advantage of others. The wicked engage in deliberate scheming and premeditated evil, not just impulsive wrongdoing. They are strategic, thoughtful, and intentional.

Gnashing teeth in Scripture signifies rage and violent resentment. This is emotional fury combined with calculated malice. Those who possess "upright conduct" are not simply ignored; they are targeted because of the threat they pose to evil schemes. Integrity provokes opposition.

The derogatory images in February of Barack and Michelle Obama illustrate the malice that is present in the hearts and minds of evildoers.

"The Lord laughs at him, For He sees that his day is coming."

The laughter of the Lord is not amusement but derision. God mocks the intentions of the wicked. He is never anxious about the schemes of evildoers, nor should we be anxious. The coming "day" refers to the appointed time of reckoning. The wicked operate on borrowed time.

"The wicked have drawn the sword And have bent their bow, To cast down the poor and needy, To slay those who are of upright conduct."

This does not speak of random violence, but targeted injustice. The wicked exploit vulnerability and exercise power with cruelty. Psalm 37 reminds us that injustice is not permanent.

"Their sword shall enter their own heart, And their bows shall be broken."

The instruments of their violence become instruments of self-destruction. We see this principle throughout Scripture: wicked people are self-destructive.

~ Haman's gallows (Esther 7)

~ Daniel's accusers (Daniel 6)

~ The principle of sowing and reaping (Galatians 6:7)

~ "Whoever digs a pit will fall into it; if someone rolls a stone, it will roll back on them" (Proverbs 26:27)

The "breaking of the bow" signifies the removal of power and capacity to harm. Evil carries the seeds of its own collapse. It is amazing how Scripture not only exposes human nature but also outlines the consequences of behavior—good or bad.

Even with difficult passages like this, we can take hope that God sees everything. He has given humans free will, so people can choose to do wrong or to do well. Those of us committed to doing well must continue shining our light.

Put another way, Jesus said that we are "the light of the world." He intends for us to shine our lights in every area of life.

The Apostle Paul wrote, *"Where sin abounded, grace much more abounded."* (Romans 5:20).

Our hope in God is always greater than the schemes of the wicked.

Reflection Question: Why is God not "stressed" about evildoers? What gives you hope?

Day 13 — How Less Can Be More

Psalm 37:16, *A little that a righteous man has is better than the riches of many wicked.*

Key Thought: More without God is emptiness.

Prayer: Teach me gratitude and sufficiency.

The word "little" does not equate to poverty. It acknowledges modest or middle-class means. Most people in the world have limited resources, influence, recognition, and limited visible success. But none of these are the factors that define personal righteousness.

What makes the "little" valuable is not the amount, but the person who possesses it and the God who sustains him. A righteous person's resources are honestly obtained, spiritually supported, and shared with others.

The Hebrew word for "better" means good, beneficial, and advantageous. The "better" that the righteous possess is dedicated to better purposes. Things that are small but blessed surpass what is great but corrupted. The righteous do not need excess to be secure.

Wicked wealth may look impressive, but it lacks divine backing. The righteous may operate in modest conditions, but they are supported by an eternal Kingdom system. Jesus Christ embodied this principle.

Ultimately, we measure our lives by faithfulness and serving others, not by accumulation.

Reflection Question: How do you measure "more" and "better?"

Day 14 — God Knows Your Days

Psalm 37:18–19, *The Lord knows the days of the upright, And their inheritance shall be forever. 19 They shall not be ashamed in the evil time, And in the days of famine they shall be satisfied.*

Key Thought: God pays attention to you

Prayer: Teach me to trust You every day, regardless of the circumstances.

"The LORD knows the days of the upright"

God cares for you, is overseeing you, and is not missing any details. We think of days in terms of calendar dates, special events, and conditions. God sees our days over the entire span of life. God sees days as seasons, including seasons of ease and seasons of hardship.

"Their inheritance shall be forever"

The Lord sees seasons because He is a generational God. The Lord was thinking about you when your great-grandparents were in the prime of their lives. Not many of us had the opportunity to know our great-grandparents, but what God put in them was also an inheritance for you. And what God is putting in you will be an inheritance for your children, grandchildren, great-grandchildren, and people with whom you relate over the course of your life.

Sometimes circumstances can make you feel insignificant, but we are all here by God's design and purpose. That's why your days are very important – it's not about a feeling. God knows your days.

Part of our inheritance is not simply material things that are handed down to us from family members. Most of our ancestors did not have the material possessions that we have today. Many had something much greater: They had faith in God, integrity, talents, and the will to overcome and succeed.

The most significant inheritance is the virtues we have from the Lord that we can leave for others. God Himself is our ultimate inheritance.

"And in the days of famine they shall be satisfied."

Famine is extreme scarcity, whether material or spiritual. Amos 8:11 reads, When I will send a famine throughout the land, not a famine of food or a thirst for water, but rather a famine of hearing the words of the Lord.

The present famine of "hearing the words of the Lord" leaves a void that material things cannot fulfill. We cannot overemphasize the importance of receiving the Word of God, being a doer of the Word, and recognizing that Jesus is the Word.

Because the inheritance is forever, we always overcome famine—whether material or spiritual—because, as Jesus said, "Seek first the kingdom of God and His righteousness, and all these things shall be added to you." (Matthew 6:33)

Reflection Question: What are some specific ways you are aware that God knows your days?

Day 15 — The End of the Wicked

Psalm 37:20, *But the wicked shall perish; And the enemies of the Lord, Like the splendor of the meadows, shall vanish. Into smoke they shall vanish away.*

Key Thought: Wickedness has an expiration date

Prayer: Fix my heart on eternal things while I address conditions in the present time

Psalm 37:20 teaches that evil is not permanent. Its seeming beauty and power are temporary because its end is disappearance. Verse 20 magnifies themes already introduced in verses 2, 9, 10, and 13. Evil has an expiration date.

"But the wicked shall perish"

As stated in previous verses, the Hebrew word for perish means lost, ruined, or brought to nothing. It does not always mean immediate physical death. It indicates loss of standing, loss of influence, and removal from covenant blessing.

"The enemies of the Lord"

This verse shifts from "the wicked" to describe those who are actively opposed to God's purposes. Being an "enemy of the Lord" is not merely personal immorality; it includes opposition to righteousness, justice, and harm toward people.

The psalm reassures those of us who serve God that our conflict is not merely with people, but with forces that resist

God's way. As Paul wrote, we don't "wrestle" (or fret with) "flesh and blood" (people). We contend with spiritual forces that manifest through people.

"Like the splendor of the meadows"

The psalmist uses this beautiful picture to describe the suddenness of the removal of the wicked. He makes reference to a lush pasture with green grass and fields in full bloom. But grass in the ancient Near East was seasonal. After rain, it flourished brilliantly, but under the heat of the sunlight, it withered quickly.

David's point: Wickedness may look vibrant and powerful, but it is seasonal. Like "smoke," the wicked and enemies of the Lord "shall vanish away." He is not describing a gradual fade, but a disappearance that leaves no trace.

Again, we do not need to worry and fret about evildoers. We should stay focused on serving God, doing His will, and serving others. We will address systems that adversely affect people, but we won't engage in warfare against people, rather against the spiritual forces that motivate them.

Reflection Question: How do you keep your heart at peace in times like these?

Day 16 — Generosity Reveals the Heart

Written by Contributor: Patricia Hudson

Psalm 37:21–22, *The wicked borrows and does not repay, But the righteous shows mercy and gives. For those blessed by Him shall inherit the earth, But those cursed by Him shall be cut off.*

Key Thought: Giving reflects trust.

Prayer: Because I have been made righteous, help me to be generous and faithful.

In Psalm 37, David contrasts the way God protects and saves His people with the ruin which awaits the wicked. He describes not only the blessings of the righteous but also their character and conduct. The Lord blesses the righteous with the promise of an inheritance, protection, provision, and His presence.

"Evil men borrow but do not repay their debt, but the godly show compassion and are generous." (Psalm 37:21).

The contrasting actions of the wicked and the righteous reveal their purpose of heart in relation to generosity.

"The wicked borrows and does not repay, but the righteous shows mercy and gives."

David concluded that the difference between the wicked and the righteous was not only found in what they believed and in whom they trusted. The difference was also often seen in their conduct. The wicked are takers, borrowing and not repaying. The righteous are givers, full of mercy.

One of the marks of a wicked person is his lack of trustworthiness. The idea is that he lives in a condition of lack that leads to borrowing but will not have the means of repaying what he has borrowed; that he will be "reckless" about borrowing and careless about paying.

In contrast, a righteous person not only meets his obligations, he practices generosity. The righteous have what they need because God blesses them, and therefore they can give to others. The righteous will not only have enough for himself, but will have the means of showing mercy to others, giving to them what they need. It is a characteristic of a righteous man that he will not borrow when he can avoid it and that he will be punctual in paying what he has borrowed.

"Surely those favored by the Lord will possess the land, but those rejected by Him will be wiped out" (Psalm 37:22).

This verse emphasizes that the righteous will receive favor, blessing, stability, and inheritance from God, while those who reject Him face destruction. The consequence of rejecting God and His ways brings all forms of despair on earth and eternal separation from God.

Reflection Question: In what ways does the heart of the righteous demonstrate generosity to others?

Day 17 — Ordered Steps, Part One

Psalm 37:23–24, *The steps of a good man are ordered by the Lord, And He delights in his way. 24 Though he fall, he shall not be utterly cast down; For the Lord upholds him with His hand.*

Key Thought: God celebrates guiding His people

Prayer: Help me to stay aligned with Your purposes

"The steps of a good man are ordered by the Lord"

"Good man" is the righteous person, one who is aligned with covenant faithfulness (see Psalm 37:18, 21).

The Hebrew word for "steps" refers to individual movements, daily decisions, progress, and life direction.

The Hebrew word for "ordered" means established, made firm, secured, and prepared.

This verse does not suggest that God directs people apart from their choices. It is stating that one of the blessings of being "good" is that we can expect God's guidance. He will not force His decisions upon us, but the Lord will give us enough insight and wisdom to make good choices. In the end, we are accountable for our choices, not God.

We learn from this text that God is actively involved in our progression through life. As Jesus said, "Seek first His kingdom and His righteousness, and all these things will be given to you" (Matthew 6:33). Living aligned with God's Word and purposes positions a person for divine establishment. Direction and stability are relational, something that comes through our relationship with God, not merely by religious deeds.

"And He delights in his way"

We talk a lot about our need to delight in the Lord, but we should also consider that the Lord wants to delight in us. "Delight" means to take pleasure in, desire, favor, and be bent toward.

God does not force guidance upon us; He takes pleasure in our path. He does not simply "tolerate" us—God celebrates His people. This reflects covenant intimacy. The believer's obedience aligns with God's purposes, and that alignment brings divine pleasure.

For Part Two, we will address "Though he fall."

Reflection Question: What does it mean to be "good" and how does that impact upon God's covenant faithfulness?

Day 18 — Ordered Steps, Part Two

Psalm 37:23–24, *The steps of a good man are ordered by the Lord, And He delights in his way. 24 Though he fall, he shall not be utterly cast down; For the Lord upholds him with His hand.*

Key Thought: God preserves the faithful

Prayer: Thank you for preserving me when I come short

If you have not done so, you would benefit from reading "Ordered Steps," Part One.

We will focus on verse 24: *"Though he fall, he shall not be utterly cast down; For the Lord upholds him with His hand."*

Those who seek to be "good" and live righteously are not above mistakes and missteps. The Hebrew word for "fall" does not imply moral collapse. People actively seeking to serve the Lord and live righteously do not become sinful and wicked. The word "fall" speaks to stumbling, temporary setbacks, and circumstantial failure.

"Whoever has been born of God does not sin, for His seed remains in him; and he cannot sin, because he has been born of God." 1 John 3:9

"He cannot sin" means wrongdoing does not come from his new creation nature in Christ. As faithful Christ followers, our "sins" ("miss the mark") have more to do with engaging in lesser standards, such as failing to pray, serve, give, etc.

Faithfulness to God does not impart perfection or eliminate vulnerability to mistakes or oversights.

Speaking to Christ followers, the Apostle John wrote in 1 John 1:7–9:

But if we walk in the light as He is in the light, we have fellowship with one another, and the blood of Jesus Christ His Son cleanses us from all sin. 8 If we say that we have no sin, we deceive ourselves, and the truth is not in us. 9 If we confess our sins, He is faithful and just to forgive us our sins and to cleanse us from all unrighteousness.

John wrote to people already walking in the light and living by higher standards. Failing to acknowledge that we all come short at times is saying, "I have no sin" or "I never come short." Living by higher standards is much different than living without concern for the higher standards of God's kingdom, where people routinely ignore God's directives to pray, serve, give, etc. Failing in these areas does not put a person at risk of losing their salvation; they simply live in the reality of not pleasing God.

"He shall not be utterly cast down"

Because we are faithful and steadfast toward God, and as much as His grace empowers us to do so, when we come short, we are not "utterly cast down." This phrase means hurled headlong, destroyed, and ruined beyond recovery.

We may fall, but we are not abandoned to ruin because we do not fall away from God. People who are good and whose steps are ordered by the Lord quickly acknowledge errors and make correction. Getting drunk, lying, or doing something ridiculous are not patterns in our lives.

This is in direct contrast to the wicked cited earlier in Psalm 37, who are "cut off" and whose "arms shall be broken" (vv. 9, 17). The wicked collapse permanently; the righteous always recover.

"For the Lord upholds him with His hand"

The Hebrew word for "upholds" means to grasp, sustain, hold firmly. The beautiful picture is of the Lord holding on to us like a parent holds his child to keep him safe, even when he stumbles.

Christ is fully engaged with His people day by day. This is why we delight in the Lord. He preserves His people; we live in covenant care and experience God's faithfulness, which is always stronger than human weakness.

Reflection Question: How do the sins of the righteous differ from the sins of the wicked?

Day 19 — A Living Testimony

Written by Contributor: Patricia Hudson

Psalm 37:25, *I have been young, and now am old; Yet I have not seen the righteous forsaken, Nor his descendants begging bread. 26 He is ever merciful, and lends; And his descendants are blessed.*

Key Thought: Faithfulness leaves a legacy

Prayer: Let my life testify to Your goodness. Lord, grant me the wisdom to convey these truths to the next generation in a way that connects them to You.

David gave a testimony from his own experience. He declares that he has witnessed and has been a recipient of the faithfulness of God. In biblical culture, age was associated with wisdom and authority, and elders were respected for their life experience. This was David's conclusion after many years of observing and experiencing that God cares for those who trust in Him and walk in righteousness.

The assurance that the righteous are never abandoned aligns with God's covenant promises throughout the Old Testament, where He pledges to be with His people. We can be confident of God's faithfulness and His commitment to those who are devoted to Him. They were not forsaken, and their descendants were also blessed. The blessings of the righteous extend to their children, emphasizing the importance of a godly legacy. This part of the verse highlights the generational blessings that come from living a righteous life.

He states, *"I have been young, and now am old; Yet I have not seen the righteous forsaken, Nor his descendants begging bread."*

Seeing God's faithfulness to His people, David wanted a younger generation to also trust in Him, learning from his wisdom. The transition from youth to old age is a common biblical theme, highlighting the faithfulness of God throughout the different stages of life. The blessings of the righteous extend to their children, emphasizing the importance of a godly legacy. This part of the verse highlights the generational blessings that come from living a righteous life.

"He is ever merciful, and lends; And his descendants are blessed."

He is ever merciful and lends: the righteous one not only receives God's provision, but with a generous and merciful heart, he lends to others in need. Psalm 37:26 celebrates the righteous as people who continually give, eagerly lend, and see their children flourish. God is faithful to provide for the righteous, and He responds by extending blessing to the next generation. This verse invites us to trust God's provision, practice active generosity, and rejoice that this same grace will touch our descendants.

Reflection Question: How is my life, what I do, more than what I say, a testimony of your goodness and faithfulness?

Day 20 — God Loves Justice

Written by Contributor: Pastor Lee Robb

Psalm 37:27-29, *Depart from evil, and do good; And dwell forevermore. 28 For the Lord loves justice, And does not forsake His saints; They are preserved forever, But the descendants of the wicked shall be cut off. 29 The righteous shall inherit the land, And dwell in it forever.*

Key Thought: Justice flows from God's character.

Prayer: Establish my life in Your justice.

Psalm 37 is written to steady believers whose faith is being tested by what they see.

- The wicked are flourishing.
- Corruption looks comfortable.
- Righteousness looks slow.

David's answer is not political strategy; it is theological clarity. We must understand that justice is not something God occasionally does. Justice flows from who God is.

David calls for righteous living before he explains divine justice. Why? Because righteousness is alignment with God's nature. If justice flows from God's character, then evil is ultimately unstable because it contradicts the moral structure of the universe.

- God's ways are not outdated.
- God's standards are not negotiable.
- God's moral order is not temporary.

You turn from evil not because evil isn't profitable, but because it is incompatible with God's character.

"For the Lord loves justice…" (v.28)

This is the hinge of the passage. David does not say, "The Lord tolerates justice," nor, "The Lord occasionally enforces justice." He says, "The Lord loves justice."

That means justice is not a reaction but an expression.

- It flows from His holiness.
- It flows from His righteousness.
- It flows from His covenant faithfulness.

If justice flows from God's character, then:

- Injustice cannot have the final word.
- Wickedness cannot have permanent footing.
- Righteousness cannot be eternally ignored.

Even when courts fail, when systems falter, when culture shifts, God's character does not change. We can learn to trust God more when we realize that God's character is eternal, but circumstances are seasonal.

Possession is opportunistic, but inheritance is covenantal. This means measuring your life by covenant promises, not by cultural trends.

At Calvary, it looked like injustice would triumph. It looked like righteousness was crushed. But justice was not ignored; it was satisfied. Mercy was not sentimental; it was secured. At the Cross, we see clearly that justice flows from God's character. Romans describes God as "just and the justifier."

The resurrection is the public declaration that God's character cannot be defeated. The Righteous One was not forsaken. And because He lives, the righteous will inherit.

Reflection question: What is your response to God when you see the world reward evil and sideline righteousness?

Day 21: Salvation Belongs to the Lord

Psalm 37:39–40, *"But the salvation of the righteous is from the Lord; He is their strength in the time of trouble. And the Lord shall help them and deliver them; He shall deliver them from the wicked, And save them, Because they trust in Him."*

Key Thought: God is always our refuge and deliverer.

Prayer: I trust You, Lord.

As we conclude this 21-day devotional through Psalm 37, let us remember this is a wisdom psalm, not a lament. David is not "venting" or expressing frustrations. He contrasts the temporary flourishing of the wicked with God's plan and provision for the righteous. Verses 39–40 serve as a summary of the entire psalm.

Some key themes we learned from Psalm 37:

- Do not fret because of evildoers (vv. 1–2)
- Trust in the Lord (v. 3)
- Delight in Him (v. 4)
- Commit your way to Him (v. 5)
- Wait patiently with expectation (v. 7)
- Meekness is not weakness (v. 11)
- The wicked will perish (vv. 9–22)
- God knows our days (vv. 18-19)

- Generosity Reveals the Heart (vv. 21-22)
- Our steps are ordered by the Lord (vv. 23–24)
- The righteous are upheld (vv. 23–24)
- God's justice prevails (vv. 27-29)

David closes this psalm by reminding us who is in charge, what God will change, and where we are headed. Our identity and security are rooted in Christ. "Greater is He who is in you than he who is in the world." (1 John 4:4)

"The salvation of the righteous is from the Lord"

David emphasizes the true source of salvation: It is "from the Lord." Salvation does not originate:

- From personal strategy
- From retaliation
- From political advantage
- From accumulated power

Systems, people, politicians, programs, and religions all promise some form of salvation—power to lift people to a better place in life. All of these may help in one way or another, but enduring salvation only comes from the Lord.

The Hebrew word for "salvation" means deliverance, rescue, victory. God's salvation is both temporal and eternal, with benefits now and the blessing of a new reality after this life. We are not limited to only longing for the "sweet by and by." God can grant some earthly heaven before heaven in the afterlife.

Do not underestimate God's ability to empower victorious living while we are still living among all the perils of the wicked. Consider the words of the Apostle Peter: Therefore, brethren, be even more diligent to make your call and election sure, for if you do these things you will never stumble; for so an entrance will be supplied to you abundantly into the everlasting kingdom of our Lord and Savior Jesus Christ. (2 Peter 1:10–11)

The "entrance" is experiencing heaven on earth while on the way to God's heaven. Note the responsibility to "make your calling and election sure," which simply means to lean into God and His kingdom.

We read in Psalm 23:5, "You prepare a table before me in the presence of my enemies; You anoint my head with oil; My cup runs over."

New Testament Scriptures confirm God's delivering nature:

Romans 8:31, "If God is for us, who can be against us?"

2 Timothy 4:18, "The Lord will deliver me from every evil work…"

"He is their strength in the time of trouble"

The Hebrew word for "strength" מ means fortress, stronghold, and a place of protection. We don't only focus on what God does, but who God is. He is not merely a rescuer; He is a refuge. We don't have a transactional relationship with God by seeking "a blessing" when we need it. We live in a covenantal relationship with God, day by day.

"He shall deliver them from the wicked, And save them, Because they trust in Him."

Remember:

- Salvation originates from God alone.
- God Himself is the refuge of the righteous.
- Trouble does not cancel covenant protection.
- Deliverance is certain, though timing may vary.
- Trust is the foundation of divine rescue and progress going forward.

Psalm 37 ends where it started: "Trust in the Lord."

I trust that you were inspired, encouraged, and educated through this 21-day journey through Psalm 37! It was a joy preparing these lessons and having contributions from Patricia Hudson, Stacy Williams, and Pastor Lee Robb.

"Every good thing happens on a Firm Foundation!"

Pastor Bryan Hudson, D.Min.

Reflection Question: What are some takeaways from this devotional that have become foundational to your life going forward?

About the Author

Bryan Hudson (D.Min.) is a pastor, author, and ministry technology consultant. He is the founding pastor of New Covenant Church & Ministries in Indianapolis, Indiana, where he has served for 44 years. Bryan operates a multimedia firm, Vision Communications, that equips people, ministries, and organizations with life-changing media and digital media solutions. He has more than 45 years' experience in media production, training, and consulting.

Bryan Hudson has earned a Bachelor of Science in Media Arts & Science from Indiana University Indianapolis, a Master of Science in Instructional Systems Technology from Indiana University, Bloomington, and a Doctor of Ministry from Andersonville Theological Seminary (a Bible school).

His education reflects his calling to serve God's purposes in ministry, media, and education. Bryan's passion is teaching the Word of God, serving everyday people, and helping Christian leaders more effectively serve their congregations and communities. For 20 years, he conducted multimedia workshops for youth that helped many enter careers as media producers. Pastor Hudson helped establish a Christian training institute in Lagos, Nigeria, Africa, and participated in fruitful missions to Kenya, Africa, in 2013, 2016, and 2018.

For 45 years, Bryan has been married to Patricia Ann Hudson (M.A.), a retired inner-city public school educator of 42 years. They have raised four children, have three grandchildren, and reside in Indianapolis, Indiana.